Their

Poetic

Minds

Books by the Anonymous Author and Artist

Poems of Life

Poems are mixed schematically, stylistically, and randomly.

Life's Heart Break: A Novella

In the end, will Zenald discover what may be one of life's biggest heart-breaks: heart-ache?

Duty & Destruction I

A real female experiences life in and out of the U.S. military.

Life's Poetic Dichotomies

Some of life's biggest dichotomies are juxtaposed poetically.

Her Poetic Rise

It is for the religiously poetic that blends religion and feminism.

Life's Short Stories

Fictional characters vie to live their own lives.

Life's Mixed Poetry

Poems are mixed schematically, stylistically, and randomly.

Life's Novellas: Fate Waits Upon No One

The good and the bad are juxtaposed, chronologically, fictionally, and theatrically.

Art Book

The Diamond & Heart Art Collections

Pictures are exhibited, categorically, by coloring schemes and coloring mediums; all of which, have been affected with special effects.

Schemes: pastel shades; earth tones; primary colors; gray, black and white; black and white.

Mediums: colored pencils; water coloring; pastel coloring; acrylic coloring; oil coloring.

Their Poetic Minds

Anonymous

Century Conquests

Their Poetic Minds

www.centuryconquests.com
info@centuryconquests.com

ISBN: 978-0-9850698-6-5

Cover graphic designed by: Century Conquests © 2013

Century Conquests ® 2012

Their Poetic Minds

Anonymous

Acknowledgements

For the small voice deep within me that still wants me to carry on poetically.

I thank every single person that has helped with the publication of this book.

I even thank every single reader of my book for permitting me the privilege. To interest, and engage, and even make clear to you: my artistic, creative, and literary reasoning.

To all vertuous Ladies in generall

Each blessed Lady that in Virtue spends
Your precious time to beautifie your soules;
Come wait on hir whom winged Fame attends
And in her hand the Booke where the inroules
Those high deserts that Majestie commends:
    Let this faire Queen not attended bee,
    When in my Glasse she daines her selfe to see....

        —Aemilia Lanyer
        (1569-1645)

A Licentious Person

Thy sins and hairs may no man equal call,
For, as thy sins increase, thy hairs do fall.

        —John Donne
        (1572-1631)

Foreword

It was right during the Renaissance, beginning in 14th-century's Florence, Italy, to 17th-century's Europe: or, more specifically, the reign of King James Stuart (1603-1649); that, an intellectual movement and an artistic movement both began, in earnest. In effect, it was all about a real renewal of life: vigor, interest, and revival—or, the Re-Birth. Equally, such era was all about one's mentality, emotionality, and physicality, and even spirituality; having been affected, if not effected, in one way, or another way, or even some other way. Almost, certainly, such influences were religious, cultural, social, and political, and even economical, and so forth, in nature; all of which, existent powers, comprised a unique power structure: mainly, a predominately religious and paternal or masculine if not sexist yet dichotomous—hierarchy: or, pecking order.

Hence, such era brought along a Female of a Feminist, or a precursory, if not a prodigious Poetess; who chose, so deliberately, and daringly, and even passionately, or religiously, yet literarily; to use the Creator's words and ways to elevate Her and other Females—or, Women: well above the digressive, regressive, repressive, oppressive, or depressive, or even successive, male-oriented—power structure, hierarchy: or, even, an un-prettily poisonous pecking order; which just assumed that Females or Women were so roundly responsible for the down-right down-fall of the human race. Such feminine or feministic elevation transpired through Aemilia Lanyer's (1569-1645) poetry and prose; whose definitely daring back-ground was the words and ways of God and Christ. Their words and ways were stressed, so femininely, and fabulously, yet fiercely; rightly, to lift Women up, most honorably, whence they had fallen, supposedly.

Right, on the other hand, such era brought along a male of a dichotomous meta-physician or poet, John Donne (1572-1631); who chose, so consciously, and boldly, and even keenly, or religiously, but dichotomously, yet literarily; to use the Creator's words and ways; to in-corporate his in-corporeal self with his corporeal self; and, even, to use such words and ways against others, or so-called sinners—and, without doubt or fail. Such transpired through his conversely clever conceits: That has captured the circularly crucial nature of life, its actuality, and its familiarity: even if, in super self-contained and super self-conceptual systems. He took, too, guilty pleasure, and, quite, in exposing the darkly damnable double-sidedness of both females and males; by just un-masking their damnably dark double-talking and double-dealing; which, led, ultimately, to either sexes or genders having been down-right double-acting; and, all, to what actual avail?

So, accordingly, religiously feministic poems right in the very spirit of what the pretty powerful Poetess—Aemilia Lanyer, advocated for: the liberation of Females, are juxtaposed; to the religiously dichotomous poems in the spirit of what the marvelously masterful meta-physician—or, John Donne, so advocated for: exposing the irreligious double-mindedness of both males and females; the last of whom, needed, so ironically, elevation, still, in spite of any kind of de-elevation whether religious or otherwise. It is, also, via my own pen—or, pencil, and design, as it were, that I have thus juxtaposed such poems in this poetry book: Primarily, to portray if not compare and then contrast the circularly; or, the conversely contrastive comparison of the two illustriously poetic writers' styles of writing, quite poetically.

Most, particularly, by way of various sorts of rhymes or even the mix thereof: masculine, feminine, and, slant, and, sometimes, perfect; rhyme schemes: aa, aba, abab, ababa, and the like; and, types of poems: couplets—aa, bb, cc, dd, and so forth; terza rimas: aba, bcb, cdc, ded, and so on; quatrains: abab, cdcd, efef, ghgh, and the like; whose dis-similarity in lines—(or, stanzas), right, in conjunction with the dis-similar rhyme schemes are, for the most part, sonnets: a mix of the time-honored, or the long-established 14 lines of poetry. Such is seen in the Spenserian sonnet: abab, bcbc, cdcd, ee; Petrarchan (Italian) sonnet: abbaabba, cdecde; Shakespearean sonnet: abab, cdcd, efef, gg. Lastly, the poems are set right to a fixed form as opposed to an un-fixed form, all through the use of such poetic devices or poetic tools. A fixed form is like a sonnet. Plus, an un-fixed form is like free-verse.

Part I

An Enthusiast

Because of God's words and ways, the Woman seeks to yoke Hope;

Only, to find out that it almost certainly can be chok'd—or, rop'd.

A Pessimist

Because of her hopelessness, she just goes on mir'd by Despair:
Like a great big female grizzly bear, that cares nothing for being the wild's would-be

heir.

True-Hearted

To make her fate come true, the woman always has hope, Faith, and ambition, and even strength, or staying power, *personal power*:

Persisting right in the merciful face of postponement;

Because of the Lord's words—alone, she'll become the woman of the hour.

Faithful

Being un-filled, his lot in life remains, roundly, in Doubt,
Withstanding its total tout, it still amounts to nil—or zip;
None of which, will stop the faith-less man from being undoubtedly devout.

Get Up and Go

On the job, the group of Females has lots of Ambition.

Nor are they ev'r scared by their fabulously fine femininity;

It almost nev'r causes them any vacillation.

This is to say—that, feminine qualities aren't allowed to bring about any

Susceptibility.

Secret Slackers

At home, the men are little more than Sloths;

    For this, their women would give a great big vouch.

While out and about, others see them as extremely energetic men on the move;

    When they're on the move, they ev'n have to be soothed.

Will Power

In her Father's words, she seizes Might,

    Seizing that which almost nev'r gets away;

Because, the power of His words and ways always greaten the width,

    Widening up and down and around, all day;

        Hence, her strength only expands way pass its initial length.

The Underbelly

In the Devil's world, the male wrestles with Weakness,

  While his ethics, morality, and character all sink into a state of nakedly dark sin;

His darkly diabolical behavior, just the same, is almost nev'r seamless,

  While at the same time, the male wishes to be on some roundly righteous mend;

Yet, he just goes on perfecting it (weakness) with such keenness.

Part II

Laying Away

Early on, the female learned the face-value of investment, or Commitment.

And, if any real deal proved, later, to have been un-timely,

It was her choice, solely, to still honor such agreement.

Double-Dealer

At church, the gentle man swears off the biggest sort of Infidelity;

When he's not at church, howev'r, he indulges whole-heartedly in perfidy or,

Treachery.

Firmness of Mind

In the end, the female wins only because of her saintly Steadfastness.

In the beginning, though, her steady purpose in life seems un-prevailing.

She, still, manages, to prevail using her own special brand of pur-pos-ive-ness—or,

Stick-to-it-ive-ness.

Throwing in the Towel

Being so tir'd of see-sawing, or zig-zagging, or even damn wig-wagging,

I'm finally calling it Quits;

But, not, before turning around, ambivalently, and witlessly, all over again.

Because, my wits have since done more than just limp'd off a bit.

Bold-Spiritedness

It's what propels the female to become a soldier—Valor;

   She'll be a fantastic fighter fighting ev'n before knowing its full consequence.

Such tour of duty will necessitate that her performance be rather stellar;

   Because, her pre-sparkling just like a super star is almost always of great

Significance!

Afraid of One's Shadow

Born and bred, at home, to be something far more than a nakedly weak Coward;

It's just that such future seems rather sour as, to make her glower and then cower.

The girl is looking—still, to her beautifully bright future yet is afraid to face it down;

And, she's bound or taken down—in-arguably, like some weakly naked clown.

Part III

Self-Possession

Since the Girl has it within herself, she hardly ev'r seeks it while out and about:
Tranquility.

Shhhh!

Because, the Divine Being's teachings almost always appease her need for
Serenity.

Tempest in a Teapot

At court, she's a colorfully and a circularly choky cloud that's pretty full of physical
Pother;
On, the other hand, when there's no up-standing man around, she dares not to bother.

Fine Fettle

I almost always exercise to improve my Health.

    While excising most unfailingly, I nev'r feel any wrath;

        But, instead, I've an abundance of my Divine Father's wealth.

Throw-Ups

His education, training, and experience, could or would nev'r be enough,

To keep it away, Sickness;

Heedless, the doctor remains quite ignorant of his own starkly or darkly if not

Deathly diagnosis;

Even as the roundly rotten growth growing inside his body grows with such

Rottenness.

Heart's Desire

It'll find me on a gorgeous yet gray but great day—love—His Love:

Like, the gently snow-white color'd bird that personifies piety and placidity—dove.

        Then, it'll always want to stay with me and nev'r go away;

Such love doesn't want to go astray, ev'r, on any day; that may leave it at bay—and,

        Not, at all, gay.

Heartbreak

The woman has begun to hate the man that's caused her such Heartache;

His love has prov'n to be fake yet somehow real but still shaky and fated.

This being why she, almost, always, feels, as if theirs is an in-escapable relationship of

A rape:

It's a not so dated or under-rated but jaded relation that should've been long ago,

Vacated.

Seventh Heaven

At work, the females almost nev'r experience any Pain;

HOORAH! It's because of their Maker's effort to keep them ache-less.

It's a small price, just, the same, that they won't have to pay for their

Super big gain.

Nor will they ev'r appear purpose-less;

Their Maker has ensur'd that the females' winnings will nev'r wane or be maim'd—

In vain.

Creature Comforts

The man almost nev'r wants it when it's available, Pleasure.

Signing, often-times, in dis-pleasure at the mere thought of it being given freely to him;

He instead steals it—pleasure, when it's un-available, howev'r, gradual.

Because, it's almost always about some super big win:

Or, the starkly dark thrill of the small steal that gives him the most

Rapture.

Well-Pleased

When she's with the man, the woman feels such Gayness.

When he touches her, she's no longer face-less.

When the man's with the woman, she nev'r feels any waywardness.

When he touches her, the woman's being is nev'r that of baseness.

When she's not with the man, she doesn't feel, at all, mate-less.

Bleeding Heart

When she's with the man, the woman feels such gladness;

When he touches her, she becomes name-less;

When the man's with the woman, she feels such Unhappiness;

When he touches her, it's by no means ache-less;

When she's not with the man, the woman just flavors all the insaneness.

Stroke of Genius

BRAVO! The ingenious Boss-Lady has always earn'd her good Fortune.

Plus, she's nev'r thought once or twice or ev'n thrice about it having been hollow:

Staying on the go; traveling high and low; and, meeting folks that haven't been, at all,

Kosher.

Indeed, it's been a long and hard yet glorious trip that others have ev'n want'd to follow;

That's right; those same folks—or, fantastic fakers are nothing but vicious yet would-be

Vouchers.

Since, they've want'd secretly to steal if not kill the Boss-Lady's power.

Checkmate

At work, you almost always try to avoid any kind of Failure.

As the company's higher-ups will hold you undoubtedly responsible and accountable;

For, the type of responsibility and accountability of your job allows for no blunder or,

Error.

If some sort of error or blunder should occur—then, you're not necessarily gone.

As such higher-ups, still, will hold you undoubtedly responsible and accountable;

For, the kind of responsibility and accountability of your job doesn't allow for another

clone—or, another damned drone.

Forward Movement

WHOOPLA! The females can now flavor a very necessary break because of their most recent Gain.

Just the same, that they can take an ev'n bigger break since they won't have to ev'r back up:

Or, go back, to a time and a place, when their darkly naked beings are lived in a big, thick, and rusty chain.

They're not about to bear any, what so ev'r, utterly un-necessary pang that's akin to being in a roundly ruinous rut;

For sure, there'll be no more living in a damn hut—being caged, like some goddamn tame game whose very life is in vain.

Just, the same, that, they aim to take that very necessary break.

On break, the females will ev'n savor a big, sweet, and blissful piece of frostily chocolate cake! HOOPLA!

Dead Loss

Take what you want or need from life, keeping in mind that it has a cost;

      Whose price may very well be a great big Loss:

A price so damn high that it'll hammer you right down,

      Begging to give back—that, which you've thus taken from life—POUND!

On the ground, being pounded around, won't be nearly enough, howev'r,

        For life to stop such pounding or exacting payment;

      As it'll only be the start-up fee for your bereavement:

An encroachment of sort, by which you take what you need or want from life;

      Such may very well be too goddamn high of a cost—or, price.

Carried Away

At church, the girl feels such Joy,

    Feeling the Prime Mover's words flow right through her soul;

Its crux is no longer cold, neither can it ev'r be bought nor sold, so she's since been told,

    Feeling His words spur her super sensational spirit to soar.

At church—still, the girl wants to soar un-like some sluggishly wild boar,

    Feeling the Prime Mover just lift her spirit;

      Its crux rather full of joy that's a beautifully bright mirror;

Seeing it toy with her light being that's now mirroring a morally up-right boy.

Millstone Round One's Neck

It's almost always about my joy and Sorrow,

Whether I've too much of one and not enough of the other;

In either case, it's almost certain that both will be right with me tomorrow.

It's, also, the latter—sorrow—whose substance just sweetens my pother.

Is it possible to have too much of one and not enough of the other?

In either case, it's almost certain that both will leave me in a few days.

It's, also, the former—joy—whose content just causes me to holler!

Again, it's almost always about my joy and sorrow;

Both of which live in the black-blue yonder—yet, visit me daily in many ways.

Part IV

Shaft of Light

It's what lightens the Woman in her darkest hour, Lightness;

For she's nev'r blind to the darkly debauch'd ways of man-kind, exhibiting maidenly

Mightiness.

Witching Hour

It's what lights up the woman's life, super striking Darkness.

But, she's still able to see what's light—or right.

Since, it (blackness) doesn't just fade away leaving her without a scratch, mark-less.

Long on Looks

At church, the female worshiper's thoughts, words, and ways are all about Rightness.

She rises up in pretty pietistic prayer, crushing, circularly, the Monarch of Hell.

Whenev'r she departs it, church, the female's full of mightiness;

She just can't help but yell while being rescued from a devilishly jet-black cell—jail.

The worshiper intends, as well, to tell anyone who'll listen to her:

That, absolutely, nothing in the Absolute's world could or would ev'r make her fail:

Not ev'n, that fantastically Foul Fiend with that diabolically dark tail.

Off Target

Because of the woman's brilliancy, there's nev'r any room for Wrongness.

She's right, too, to keep up the damn fight when others try to wrong her.

Just the same, that her brilliance is what almost always causes her loneness.

If she'd just accept some man's roundly romantic dare:

Then, there'll be quite possibly a right and a wrong—or,

A romantically un-ev'n pair.

Since the woman could or would nev'r consider lessening her rightness;

As such, stance is only fair:

Lest she just wants to end up quite sightless.

Big-Heartedness

At church, the Female pastor preaches Goodness,

  For it gives her an intense sense of fullness.

    At work, the pretty pastor ev'n takes pride in what's good;

It's easy to do so, because, she, almost, always, sports a moralistically righteous hood.

At court, all that isn't good nev'r saps the strength of her character, or chastity:

  It's the type of no-good that's still hooded with integrity or, continuity.

    At church, once again, the female pastor just preaches away;

Because of her morality and purity whilst at work, church, and court—or play.

Black-Hearted

At play, the class of men almost certainly is oblivious of their

Badness;

Living their lives both haphazardly and promiscuously:

It leaves them, in the end, so full of sadness.

In the suspicious eyes of their women, such is seen and felt most conspicuously;

Living their lives with weak and foolish men:

It leaves them, the women, in the end, quite mad and sad, obviously.

In the blind eyes of their men, they again can't and won't see their own dark sins;

Living their lives as starkly if not darkly foolish and weak men, sinners:

It leaves them un-able to bend—or win, and then be on the mend—in the end.

Far-Sighted

The aged lady is thankful for her Saneness.

YIPPEE! It's almost certainly enough to keep her moving.

It's more than enough, also, to keep her from straying and remaining blameless.

Others, irreligiously, wish that she couldn't—wouldn't do such so coolly, or smoothly.

The same aged lady is ev'n more grateful for her soundness' loudness:

It's much easier to do her towing or sowing.

Others see such as an aged lady, whose life is that of utter un-soundness.

Still, she just loves to shout out—WOW!

It's because of the kow-towers—old and jealous and un-godly men—or others that like

Kow-towing.

They almost always in secret and invisibly bow to the aged lady;

Since her sanity is always here and nev'r gone by tomorrow.

It's only the great big bond between her pre-destined joy and her non-existent sorrow.

Not Quite Right

The young woman is well aware of her Madness.

`   For it's enough to keep her coming and going;

It ev'n gives her a measure of gladness.

            That, she often-times likes doing such crazy sowing.

For, the young woman feels as if she's in another world—or, the real world;

        It's in the depths of such darkly deranged world—again, where she likes towing.

Yet, what the woman doesn't know is that her world is really a dark, deep, and

                    Dangerous hell.

            Though, it's still where she's most at home, alone.

It all just makes the young woman want to yell; she may very well not live to tell—that,

        Nothing in her world of a cell or a jail has ev'r been well!

Just, the same, that the young woman dare not dream of ev'r leaving her place of abode;

            Since, it's taken hold of her like wide, thick, and black mold.

                It dares not dream of ev'r letting the young woman go—OH NO!

Moving Force

HOORAY! The lovely pair of lovers loves living their Life.

The female lover almost certainly considers herself a colorfully celestial catch.

And, their love almost nev'r causes either of them any strife.

It's just another sure sign that their love's a heavenly match;

The lovers' lot in life mandates as much:

That, neither of them ends up alone nor be an utterly un-lovable toad.

Just the same, that the male lover trusts—that, all of life's toll roads will be pav'd with love and such.

The female lover ev'n trusts that such will nev'r turn to dark mold or get cold or ev'n grow old.

Plus, the lovers' love can only add warmth to such love.

It's lovability that always warms up the mere metal of their latch.

That the lovers, lovably, circularly, and conscientiously clasp.

Because of it—metallic fastener, the lovers almost always find themselves in the above.

To be sure, the pair of lovers' lovely love—or, match, has only just begun to hatch.

Yet again, the lovable pair of lovers loves living their life.

They just love each other while the female lover relishes being blessed beautifully.

Or, she's so very blessed to just be the love of the male lover's life or even his most heavenly wife.

The Great Adventure

Quite full of life, the wealthy haves are almost ready for its ending—Death.

Should the wealthy also care about their damnably dying fame?

Needless to say, that they're rather reluctant to leave behind their wealth;

Since its acquisition has caused them such damn pain.

Yes, indeed, the haves have been badly maimed.

Fortunately, though, such sweetly sour pang is lessened by their power;

It's the type of power that's almost always needed for them to be tamed:

Be so just like a poisonously black flower.

And, it dares not holler…!

Being so near death, the dark flowers—or, haves, could sure use another hour to flower their fantastically fallible fates.

It'll be time used not for prayer but instead to just wallow;

They'll bother to indulge their hates having transpired on certain dates, and, with certain or utterly un-celestial mates.

Quite full of life, the wealthy have-nots are now ready for its ending—hell;

It's only another place of abode where they'll live deliberately well.

That's like a dark, deep, and dirty, and even dangerous, yet delicious jail of a cell.

References

Smith, A.J.; Tobin, John. *John Donne. The Complete English Poems*. London: The Penguin Group, Inc., 1996.

Woods, Susanne. *The Poems of Aemilia Lanyer. Salve Deus Rex Judaeorum*. New York; Oxford: Oxford University Press, Inc., 1993.

www.ingramcontent.com/pod-product-compliance
Lightning Source LLC
Chambersburg PA
CBHW080938040426
42443CB00015B/3459